AURORA RISING

AN ORACLE FOR LIGHTWORKERS,
WAYSHOWERS AND DREAMERS
OF THE NEW DAWN

KATRINA SMITH

BLUE ANGEL®
PUBLISHING

AURORA RISING
An Oracle for Lightworkers, Wayshowers
and Dreamers of the New Dawn

Copyright © 2026 Katrina Smith

Published by Blue Angel Publishing®
10 Trafford Court, Wheelers Hill,
Victoria, Australia 3150
E-mail: info@blueangelonline.com
Website: www.blueangelonline.com

Edited by Cherise Asmah and Peter Loupelis

Blue Angel is a registered trademark of Blue Angel
Gallery Pty Ltd.

ISBN: 978-1-922574-56-5

FSC
MIX
Paper
FSC® C007683

Printed on sustainably sourced paper,
with soy-based inks.

CONTENTS

Welcome to the
AURORA RISING
Oracle

A LUMINOUS AWAKENING IS DAWNING across Earth. As light beings and wayshowers, we are being catalysed into our greatest becoming.

An exquisite mind-body-heart transformation is igniting across the globe as we rise into the next octave of our divine potential. A sacred alchemy is stirring. We are remembering ourselves and our true origins as the veils continue to soften. As a vessel of the divine, you are here to radiate your most brilliant light. As your luminosity expands, you become a living beacon, a radiant force field of love. Together, humanity is rising, glowing within our collective aura — an atmosphere of grace. And yet, this brilliance doesn't shine alone. As each heart answers its soul's calling, Earth is enlivened by a new paradigm — one born from devotion, intention and the awakening of our original light. At this time of great change, we are tuning in to the magnificent realms of consciousness all around us.

The *Aurora Rising* oracle supports your journey of empowerment and self-discovery. It is an open gateway to your higher knowing and all of the answers that are already within you. This deck is an extension of your light, reflecting and reminding you who you truly are. A sounding board to bounce off and gain instant clarity on your path. It is a means to cultivate a depth of intimacy with your soul. As you continue to work with the deck, you strengthen your relationship with the wisdom within. Synergy is born between your heart, mind, body and spirit, unlocking access to infinite possibilities.

.
.
.
.
.

The Realms of Aurora

As you rise into your highest potential, the subtle yet powerful essence of Aurora is with you, holding you in its ethereal luminosity. May you bask in the formless rays of pastel light, becoming enveloped within the realms of soft opalescence. The spirits of Aurora reassure you that these times of great change are in alignment with the grander cosmic orchestration that is underway. A new dawn is breaking, gently stirring what has long lain dormant within.

This is the spectrum of soul awakening: love, ascension and the rising of the luminous human.

By opening our hearts, we expand our horizons, aligning with the unseen support that surrounds us. We receive the cosmic love of Aurora, restoring every cell of our bodies and uplifting our vibrant emanation of light.

If you are here, you are not alone. You are among the lightworkers and luminaries who are rising. Your heart is glowing as love takes the lead, revealing the way forward. As we transform from human to divine human, we rise into the embodiment of what is truly possible. As we strengthen our own light source, we unite with others, igniting endless possibilities for love's manifestation on Earth.

Welcome home, lightworkers, wayshowers and all those who wish to amplify their Aurora light!

Katrina's Visual Codes

This deck holds 44 powerful visions, each crafted with layered intention, inspired by the unseen realms to which we are all intrinsically connected. Each card is a visual activation intended to be an energetic transmission in and of itself. Throughout this creation journey, I have called upon only the purest frequency imagery — photographs infused with textures, elements and tones of the natural world: water, light and plasma, the fluid medium of the realms of creation. The works reflect a deep commitment to the organic substance and the divine essence of who we truly are. The Aurora hues of soft, pearlescent colour guide us on a journey of deep nourishment. Their presence reminds us of the true strength within softness, kindness and grace. As you breathe open your heart, every space within you is filled with the essence of purity and unconditional love. I encourage you to sit with each card, to spend time allowing the imagery to reveal itself in deepening layers. These are sacred codes that broadcast from the higher creational realms and through many dimensions and levels of the self.

.
.
.
.
.

Working with the 'Aurora Rising' Oracle

This deck is a platform of empowerment — a sacred tool for intimate communion with your soul, a dialogue with your deepest knowing. Remember, you are the Source, and the Source is within you. There is nothing to seek outside of yourself. All ancient wisdom lives within you. It is the field of consciousness with all the answers to your questions. See these 44 cards as a way to connect the threads of your experience — an extension of your own inner landscape, spread out before you. Create a ceremonial space of introspection when using the deck. Flow the linear mind down into the heart as you open a portal of possibility. Let go of attaching to the outcome. A card you pull may be crystal clear or may take time to brew and land deeper. Working with our unconscious mind, its effect is multi-layered and ongoing. Allow the message of your soul to integrate physically, emotionally and mentally. Take your time and be open to the unfolding and the synchronicities that ignite in your life.

Reading for Other People

If reading the deck for others, ensure that you are neutral — this means setting aside all influence, personal will or projection upon the reading. The clearer your field, the more precise the reading will be. As the reader, you are assisting others to connect directly with their own soul. This means being deeply reverent and in devotional service. It is important to allow the process to unfold naturally without impacting the outcome.

Opening Your Sacred Space

As with all spiritual practices, setting the space is important. It sets the underlying tone for the experience about to unfold. This is something I do before all client sessions, workshops and presentations. The more heart awareness you hold, the more the field corresponds to you, supporting you in your greatest becoming.

Some suggestions for setting your space:

Choose a place that is quiet and comfortable. This could be your home, meditation corner or a space by your altar. Avoid public places that are busy with other people's energy, such as cafes or libraries.

Before opening the *Aurora Rising* oracle, take a deep breath and connect with your heart, mind and body. Invite your soul's awareness to awaken to the presence of the moment. Orient yourself to the here and now by letting go of the linear mind and tuning in to your heart's vibration. In doing so, you will flow deeper into the subtle domains of intuition, the perfect space to commune with your soul. With intention, place the deck upon your heart and ask to open the gateways to the highest good. Ask for your soul to come forward to support you.

The calling to create this oracle deck arose after years of energy healing and therapy sessions, assisting people all over the world with uniting their higher soul aspects and expanded consciousness. The 'healing' work is rather a process of remembering that you're already whole, healed and connected on every divine level. We are simply reminding ourselves what we allowed ourselves to forget. *Aurora Rising* is the bridge between forgetfulness and eternal remembrance. This is available to every divine soul, no matter which stage of the journey we are at.

It is my deepest prayer that all beings remember the truth of their own divinity. May we each rise into the exquisite majesty of our own miraculous nature — for we are miracles creating miracles.

Aurora Rising Card Spreads

Here are some suggested card spreads that you can use. Feel into what resonates most with how you feel in the present moment. This will depend on what kind of guidance you are seeking, how much time you have, or what may best suit the person you are reading for.

ONE-CARD SPREAD: Daily Guidance
This is a single-card spread that is perfect for quick guidance and clarification.

Shuffle the cards. Connect with your heart and ask your question. I like to feel my intention and energy infusing with the deck, as I remain centred and neutral towards the outcome. Spread the cards before you. Trust your intuition — let your hand be drawn to the card that calls to you most. This is your message for today.

TWO-CARD SPREAD: What Is Current / What Is Emerging
This spread is wonderful for clarifying where you're at now and where you're heading on your

path. This is a great option for getting clear and confident on the journey that's unfolding.

Shuffle the cards. Take a moment of quiet introspection. As you breathe into your heart centre, invite your higher self's presence to the space. Expand your aura of light to encompass the deck, and feel that you are one — one body of consciousness.

Lay all the cards out in front of you and allow your intuition to pull you towards your first card. Set it aside. Then, select your second card. Place these two cards face down in front of you.

Gather up the rest of the cards into a pile and set them aside. Then, turn your chosen cards face up.

The first card represents what is present. This relates to what is currently emerging in your journey and that which is asking for deeper contemplation. The second card represents what is in motion as you move towards specific changes in your life — perhaps a different mindset or outlook on life or alternative approaches to life's challenges.

THREE-CARD SPREAD: The Light / The Veil / The Becoming

This spread is perfect for in-depth soul dialogue and opening to receive comprehensive guidance. It's a great option for bringing clarity and understanding to specific themes in your life that may be more ongoing in nature. This spread offers three angles of awareness, much like the past, present and future, encompassing a broader scope of intuitive wisdom and support on how best to navigate this experience.

Shuffle the cards.

Take a deep breath, centring yourself in the heart space. With intention, ask your higher self to co-create with you and guide you now. Gently expand into your subtle awareness of self, opening to receive the messages that are in the highest alignment. Consciously release all anticipation or attachment to a specific outcome.

Lay all the cards out in front of you as you open to being naturally drawn to your first card. Set this card aside. Take a breath before continuing, feeling your hand magnetised towards your second card. Set this card aside. Then, when you're ready, take a moment to select your third card. Place these three cards face down in front of you.

Gather up the rest of the cards into a pile and set them aside. Then, turn your chosen cards face up.

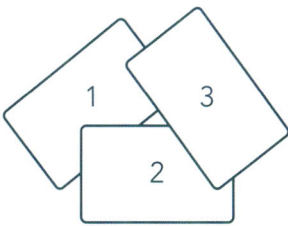

The first card represents what is known. This may be an aspect of the journey you are already aware of but requires a deeper understanding. The second card represents what is hidden. This could be something that is concealed, a blind spot asking for illumination. The third card represents what's unfolding. This card supports your understanding of the bigger picture of what you are working towards.

CARD
MESSAGES

AETHER

Transparency. Clarity. Clear Communication.

AETHER

Transparency. Clarity. Clear Communication.

You are on a journey of authenticity. You are discovering your innermost truth and sharing it with the world. Your voice is a blessing, and it is time to be raw, open and honest with yourself and others.

This card is confirmation that your sacred voice is activating, broadcasting the sound of your soul. No longer are you interested in persuasion or conforming to popular opinion. You are unique, and you see things differently. It is time for your spirit to shine, to be witnessed in all its glory.

This may shake things up in relationships, family or work situations, but this is part of building inner trust with yourself. Perhaps in the past, your feelings and opinions were not prioritised. Perhaps you adapted your inner truth to fit in. Yet pleasing others to avoid ruffling feathers no longer feels like a path you can sustain. Self-love is now at the forefront of your life. Honest, clear communication assists all involved, bringing light to spaces of disharmony and misunderstanding. Authenticity clears the filters that keep us bound in a spell, diminishing our sense of freedom and connection with others.

You are now being called to unleash your divine voice, to speak your truth, even if your voice quivers. Allow the trembles to be felt with deep compassion for your sensitive soul. In doing so, blockages and stagnant energy can begin to shift. Take a breath, and speak from the heart. You've got this.

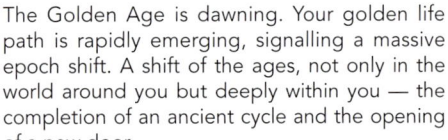

AGE OF AQUARIUS
Abundance. Soul Prosperity. Divine Flow.

AGE OF AQUARIUS

Abundance. Soul Prosperity. Divine Flow.

The Golden Age is dawning. Your golden life path is rapidly emerging, signalling a massive epoch shift. A shift of the ages, not only in the world around you but deeply within you — the completion of an ancient cycle and the opening of a new door.

This transition is calling you to explore your heart's greatest joy and passion. If finances were taken care of, what would you love to do? How would you love to show up? Release the reasoning mind. Let go of unnecessary control. It is not your job to micromanage the universe. Your freedom comes only through trust in the grander orchestration and relinquishing of all fears.

You are prosperous at the blueprint level of your existence. Abundance doesn't come to you; it comes through you. Release all illusions of lack and scarcity, the feeling of never having enough. The divine is your golden supply and overflows from the fountain of your enlivened heart. The Golden Age is within you. Act as if you have already received all the blessings you have asked for; ponder the miracles on your journey of awakening — even in the smallest or 'mundane' things. Whatever you have asked of the universe, invest yourself in preparation for its arrival, regardless of whether it has shown up yet. Ask for what you need and be liberal with the details. If it is in divine alignment, it is already done. It is time to surrender and leave it in the hands of Spirit.

ANCESTRAL LINES

Breaking Generational Patterns. Legacy of Light.

ANCESTRAL LINES

Breaking Generational Patterns. Legacy of Light.

You are a divine human being who has incarnated here on Earth with an incredible soul mission. With many lifetimes of training and preparing for this present experience, you are coded for this. As the future generation of your ancestral lines, you are paving the way for a new wave of light.

If you are the 'black sheep' of your family, you may have always felt different — seeing through a unique lens, highly sensitive and acutely aware. This is a divine gift, although you might have felt outcast and misunderstood. This card is assurance that you are breaking ancient ancestral chains, lightening the load for your lineage of light. As a powerful path cutter, you are clearing the way for new creations to be realised — a new direction of soul-led living on Earth.

This is part of your higher soul contract to transmute old patterns, beliefs and traumas that may have been unresolved or unremedied throughout the generations — only to resurface down the line. You are reminded that you are the answer to your ancestors' prayers; you heard their clarion call, and you are here.

As you continue to rise, you manifest new potentials of freedom, joy and abundance. These new codes of light illuminate entirely new realities, shining through all your unique offerings to the world. You are paving the way. You are the legacy of light.

ANCIENT MU

Soul Wisdom. Parallel Lives. Guidance Within.

ANCIENT MU

Soul Wisdom. Parallel Lives. Guidance Within.

Ancient memories are awakening within you. What was once dormant is now rising to greet you from within. Gateways are opening, drawing your awareness inward. This is more than a feeling; it's an inexplicable knowing guiding you through the dark night. When you have been feeling lost at sea, these shimmering star maps have faithfully guided you across the ocean of life, navigating your soul's voyage. Much like the celestial bodies, your cells hold the living records of your many incarnations. These constellations shine an unspoken language of light, directing your journey. They remind you of who you truly are and your place within the big picture of reality. They are the ancient codes and keys of your cosmic makeup — an unbreakable bond to the truth of your soul.

At this time of great change, you are remembering. Gentle whispers are calling you home. You know you have been here before. You are connected to a web of awakening souls who are also rising. Together, that which had been erased from history is being rewritten, braided and woven through your DNA as the light lines of your ancient past — a past linked to the future. This access is within you. It is time to honour the wisdom held within you.

ANKH

Master Keys. Soul Blueprint. Unlocking the New.

You hold the master keys for your awakening — for your highest potential. These keys open doors to entirely new realities, activated at moments of great transition in your life. Only that which is truly valuable is carefully guarded — the watchful eye of your higher self greatly assisting your way, reassuring you to only take action when the timing is right.

Perhaps the old version of self wasn't quite ready for what was on the other side of the door. Yet, with your recent soul growth, you may now find yourself at a tipping point, the bridge between the old self and the new self. Your soul's keys are time-coded, specifically corresponding to the right moment for you to shift timelines. After all, each key is an open portal to a new version of yourself.

Forcibly trying to open locks that don't match your keys causes frustration, disappointment and confusion. Force implies distrust and disconnects us from the higher energies in motion that are always working in our favour. Stop pushing for things to happen; allow the opportunities to come to you by acting and living in authenticity. Trust that all that is meant for you is on its way.

AURORA RISING
The New Era. Grid Keepers. Shared Light.

AURORA RISING

The New Era. Grid Keepers. Shared Light.

Your location is no coincidence. You are anchoring potent energy through your soul's light. As a living conduit of the divine, you are an acupuncture point, streaming higher frequencies into the New Earth grids. Your transmission is tremendous as you pulse harmonising currents everywhere you go. Just as you honour the planet, she honours you, holding you within her soothing hubs of Aurora light.

A new day is dawning, and Aurora Earth is rising. As you embody your higher self, the planet embodies hers — micro to macro, we rise together. Our planet's energy body is much like ours, for she is a living being with a spiritual presence. Life force courses through her meridians, grid lines and channels of light, and her cellular memory lives on throughout her terrain.

As you roam her lands, you are a prayer in motion, assisting the global rebirth that is underway. You circulate a potent wave of healing light by reigniting your inner light source, which is felt deeply by the earth. Ceremonial rituals such as burying crystals, meditating in nature or connecting with the elements strengthen your deeper union. As humanity heals its bond with the Great Mother, she morphs into her most miraculous form yet — Heaven on Earth. Recently, you may have felt guided to shift locations, travel abroad or relocate, as much is shifting at this time. Allow the whispers on the wind to guide you forward. Aurora New Earth is calling you.

AURORA ROSE
Purity. Intimacy. Devotion.

AURORA ROSE

Purity. Intimacy. Devotion.

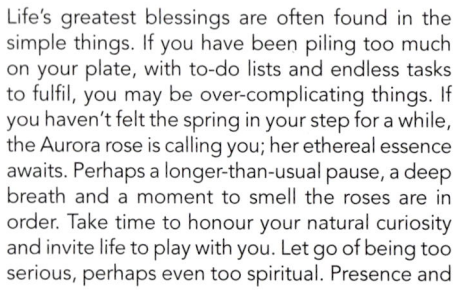

Life's greatest blessings are often found in the simple things. If you have been piling too much on your plate, with to-do lists and endless tasks to fulfil, you may be over-complicating things. If you haven't felt the spring in your step for a while, the Aurora rose is calling you; her ethereal essence awaits. Perhaps a longer-than-usual pause, a deep breath and a moment to smell the roses are in order. Take time to honour your natural curiosity and invite life to play with you. Let go of being too serious, perhaps even too spiritual. Presence and stillness draw you into the sweet spot — a place where nectar flows in unimaginable abundance.

When you are in devotion to life, you move as a prayer in motion, a walking meditation, sensitively attuned to the wonder of creation. This is the beauty that shines in the finer details as each footstep kisses the earth with gratitude. You are reminded that your life is your garden, and you are the gardener. It is time to sow the seeds of your highest self so your intentions can thrive into full bloom. When did you last tend to your garden? Perhaps it's time to pull out the overgrown weeds and turn the soil. Or maybe it is time to stake and support the new seedlings so they can rise upward to the light!

COSMIC CLOCK

Divine Timing. Patience. The Timeless Mystery.

COSMIC CLOCK

Divine Timing. Patience. The Timeless Mystery.

Timing is everything. If there is something you are wishing into your life, it may be holding back, awaiting divine timing to reveal itself. This is the great mystery of the universe and an invitation to surrender — to let go of attachment to the outcomes. Trust that if it hasn't arrived yet, it's not the right time. Perhaps more preparation is needed to get ready to receive what you have asked for. Or maybe what you have asked for, you aren't quite ready to hold just yet. It could be that the delay is serving a deeper purpose for your spiritual growth.

Our universe moves in cycles and spirals. As life lessons circulate, new opportunities are revealed — deconstructed layers with new details emerge. New angles and perspectives bring deeper meaning and understanding. You are shifting through old patterns and easing into deeper self-love. Do not be disheartened if a life lesson you had already faced in the past cycles around again. Often, we feel we're "done and dusted", yet initiations are multi-layered. You are being gifted opportunities to display your knowledge of these lessons and your heightened self-awareness. The universe reminds you to let go of trying to "get the job done" and instead celebrate your growth, layer by layer, cycle by cycle.

CRYSTAL SKULL

Knowledge. Insight. Cosmic Awakening.

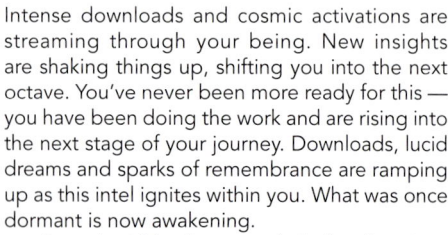

Intense downloads and cosmic activations are streaming through your being. New insights are shaking things up, shifting you into the next octave. You've never been more ready for this — you have been doing the work and are rising into the next stage of your journey. Downloads, lucid dreams and sparks of remembrance are ramping up as this intel ignites within you. What was once dormant is now awakening.

Stored within the crystal skulls of ancient times past, the memory of an awakened Earth was lovingly preserved — the living records of what is truly possible for a thriving, harmonious humanity. As this long-prophesied time is now upon us, you are being activated — along with the many gifts, special abilities and perceptions you may not have been aware you held, until now. This is the culmination of your many lifetimes lived on this planet. As your soul's memories emerge, you are reassured that you are ready. There's nothing to fear.

By staying grounded, you hold a steady mental and emotional foundation, which brings an air of calm to moments of rapid awakening. If you're wondering how to make sense of it all, now is a perfect time for intuitive writing and journalling. Allow the mind to release its analytical grip by softening into the ancient wisdom of the heart. As your memory vault unlocks, now is a delicate time of integration. Breathe, relax and trust in the process.

DARK MATTER

Divine Feminine Rising. The Fertile Domains.

Where does your soul's spark of light originate? From where is it birthed?

Dark matter is the feminine dimension, the deepest domain of raw, abundant life force. She is the primordial vastness holding the potential for all expression. Just as all life emerges from the darkness—a seed from the soil, an infant from the womb—an entire universe is birthed from the dark. Without the backdrop of darkness, we'd never see a starry night. We'd never witness the magnificence of our brilliant creations.

The seer, the psychic and the mystic are alive within you. It is time to relax the mind and allow sensation to guide you. By listening to your body, you attune to the sacred voice of the soul deep within your cells. You decode the language of spirit within. Invite your body to take the lead, to get the creative juices flowing. Unstructured movement, dance and intuitive stretching support you in releasing control and invoking your raw, spontaneous self. As you close your eyes, the inevitable darkness will always return, and along with it, the astonishing palette of possibilities — for you are the visionary artist with a brush in hand. You always were.

DARK NIGHT OF THE SOUL

Initiation. Timeline Collapse. Growing Pains.

You are in a dismantling phase. This is the collapsing of old energies and realities, as that which no longer aligns naturally fades away. Just as an old, decaying building is demolished into dust, a new architectural masterpiece is made in its place. Our growth is determined by our willingness to let go of old creations and the identities that are entwined within them. Relationships may feel like musical chairs, where friends, lovers and partners are rapidly shifting. Trust deeply in the higher plan by allowing the old layers to dissolve.

It is time to release the grip of the way things were, releasing the comfort of the familiar. Change is uncomfortable, yet your growth depends on it. The unknown is your greatest ally; it is the infinite realm of all possibility. For in the darkness comes the rebirth. You may feel the uncertainty of being in between realms, where your reality is rapidly dismantling, yet the new manifestations aren't here just yet. This is the holding phase of the great pause, the space between the inhalation and exhalation.

Old creations or commitments may no longer feel as meaningful as they once did. Create space to grieve; gently allow yourself to part ways with the old version of you. We must be willing to let go before the new energies can take shape. It is time to cease negotiating with the universe, to unravel and let go of that which is now expired. It is time to trust and welcome the new trajectory that is unfolding.

DISCLOSURE

Awareness. Revelation. Shadows Surfacing.

DISCLOSURE

Awareness. Revelation. Shadows Surfacing.

What was once hidden is now coming to light. Truths long buried are rising to the surface, emerging in the radiance of your soul's phenomenal light.

You are riding an immense wave of change, as illumination reveals all.

For healing to begin, we must be aware of our unconscious, even that which escapes our everyday notice. Awareness is light, seeping through our deepest layers and scars. It is the reviving force of the divine, piecing together the shards. As our sun intensifies its bursts of love, you, too, are being illuminated, infused with the light potentials of a new paradigm. This floods the darker caverns and crevasses of the unconscious, dislodging denser emotions and beliefs and accelerating our transformation. This alchemical shift calls you into compassionate love and acceptance for all parts of yourself.

If you have been feeling anxious or reactive lately, this card is reassurance that more is to be disclosed; more details are being revealed. Accepting your fears, doubts and insecurities alchemises them back into love, their original creation state. This frees up energy to fuel your highest life vision. Avoiding your shadows may amplify your triggers, as your soul speaks louder in the hope of catching your attention.

Remember, you are human — perfectly imperfect, learning and unlearning. It is time for the shadows to rise into the light.

DIVINE NEUTRALITY
Forgiveness. Releasing Burdens. Holding Your Centre.

DIVINE NEUTRALITY

Forgiveness. Releasing Burdens.
Holding Your Centre.

You hold the golden key to your divine heart. The royal seat of your soul connects and unites all things. In the heart, everything makes 'sense'. Your heart holds steady amid great turmoil. When in neutrality, you remain connected to the whole; it is your zero point from which spirals the eternal universal perspective. It is the spaciousness of a deep breath when all else is constricting.

When pulled out of your centre through irritation or reaction, this access becomes stifled.

The breath shallows and triggers easily push our buttons. It is time to see through the eyes of your heart to release all friction and turbulence. Blaming, criticising or judging another forms a density that we carry. They are chains of our own binding. The arrows we shoot at another shoot right back at us in covert and unpredictable ways. Wishing well for others and sending genuine blessings of love lightens the load for all involved. Be generous with forgiveness, for this liberates your own heart. Care deeply, but do not carry what is not yours to hold.

DIVINE UNION

Inner Harmony. Balance. Healing the Split.

You are being called into harmony to bring balance into your life. As a divine soul, your inner masculine and feminine are both essential for spiritual balance. While the masculine pursues and plans for the end result, the feminine creatively flows, enjoying the unfolding journey. When these energies harmonise, a united front is formed, unlocking your greatest empowerment.

Without this happy marriage within, our energy destabilises, leading to chaos in both our inner and outer worlds. This can play out in volatile relationships with ourselves and others or lead to creative longing or physical burnout.

Ask yourself: How is my inner feminine? Do I flow with my fluid, natural pace, honouring ways to express my creative energy? Does intuition magnetise me towards joyous, playful experiences? How is my inner masculine? Do I honour the structure, drive and organisation I need to fulfil my desires and projects?

It is time to synergise both mind and body in an enduring bond of trust and communication, a field rich in both electric thought and magnetic feeling. Rather than choosing one state over the other, it's a matter of tuning into what you need each day. This is the cosmic dance within you, a divine union sparked within your heart. All is one. Hand to hand, heart to heart, it's time to heal the split.

EARTHSEED
Guardianship. Elemental Support. Embodiment.

EARTHSEED

Guardianship. Elemental Support. Embodiment.

You are mothered and held by the earth. Her oceans, mountains and forests are a cherished gift to your senses, an ancient transmission of love. You are one of her divine children, and her bountiful garden is your playground. Gravity reminds you of your deepest belonging as she draws you into her core.

She whispers gently upon the winds, sending animal allies to greet you. Infused within the elements, her essence is always available to you. This card confirms you are a steward of this planet.

You are one who feels her terrain, her vibration, her pulse—two hearts beating as one—for you are an extension of her earthly body.

Drawing upon the energy of the elements is a potent way to uplift your spirits and provide direction on your path. Now is a time to rekindle your relationship with the natural world, to dedicate time to stroll through her forests and bathe in her waters, to be nurtured by the elemental realms. Gathering flowers, shells and feathers for your altar or simply adorning your space are powerful ways to connect with her frequency. In deepening your devotion, you open and receive her abundant soul medicine. Mother Earth is with you; she is calling you home.

EMERGING

Rising. Transforming. Out of the Comfort Zone.

EMERGING

Rising. Transforming. Out of the Comfort Zone.

This is a moment of great transformation. You are shedding an old cocoon that has become too tight, too constricting of your expanding light. It may feel like you're wearing a pair of shoes that no longer fit — it's uncomfortable and hinders your stepping forward. Is your cocoon holding and supporting you, or is it shrouding your growth? Is this membrane built upon walls of distrust, pain or aversion to life? This card is confirmation to feel into your heart and to clarify your motivations.

If you have been in your cocoon for a while, perhaps it may be time to test the skies, to spread your wings. It might be time to try something new, to invite in experiences that are out of the comfort zone of your day-to-day routine. In order to truly know our potential, we first must trust that we have wings, carrying us on the winds of change — to have faith in our true essence that emerges from deep within us.

You are reminded that you are now safe to be all that you are. You are safe to be free. Take a deep breath, and ask yourself, is it time to emerge from the sheath?

FIRE WATER

Alchemy. Transmutation. Back to the Dust.

What have you been holding on to that is long overdue for release?

Harbouring and holding on to past hurts stifles your inner freedom. Attachment to old stories and experiences congest and cloud your soul's clarity. This tarnishes your lenses and blurs your ability to see clearly. Holding on to reactivity and pain reinforces suffering and cords of entanglement. Wherever you have felt betrayed or hurt by another person or situation, it is time to allow the alchemising flames to rejuvenate your being — to transform and transmute this density. Return it to the dust. Breathe into your heart and surrender all blame, judgement and disappointment. It is time to incinerate all heaviness, to let go of the weight of the past.

Through radical forgiveness, your inner light is ignited; your heart bursts open in its full flowering. Be intentional with what you are ready to release and feel the diamond liquid flames engulfing and transforming it now. It is time to free up this energy and create space for the new.

GALACTIC MIRROR

Reflections. Impressions. Blind Spots.

GALACTIC MIRROR

Reflections. Impressions. Blind Spots.

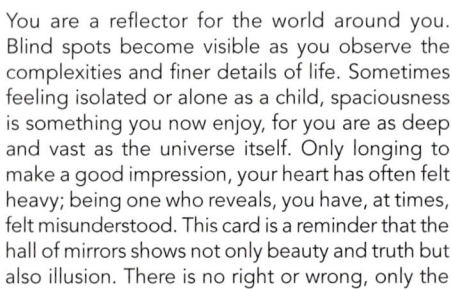

You are a reflector for the world around you. Blind spots become visible as you observe the complexities and finer details of life. Sometimes feeling isolated or alone as a child, spaciousness is something you now enjoy, for you are as deep and vast as the universe itself. Only longing to make a good impression, your heart has often felt heavy; being one who reveals, you have, at times, felt misunderstood. This card is a reminder that the hall of mirrors shows not only beauty and truth but also illusion. There is no right or wrong, only the image of what is. Avoiding the mirror, many are apprehensive to see what's being reflected back to them. Not all are ready to meet with themselves. And yet, those who are receptive lean in closer for a better view.

You are here to shine and reflect all that must be seen. One glance at a time, you are the cosmic feedback for an awakening world. Many see themselves in you. You are a familiar vibration. Your silvery aura offers a glimpse of the Great Mystery, the reflection of things as they truly are. Your eyes are open windows to the immeasurable vastness. You pierce through illusions and dissolve the veils around you. It is time to honour one of your most sacred gifts and reclaim your timeless wisdom.

GENESIS
Intentions. Seeds of Creation. Fertile Mind.

GENESIS

Intentions. Seeds of Creation. Fertile Mind.

Intentions harmonise our inner and outer worlds. They are the organising force arranging our deepest soul desires into manifestation. Now is the time to get clear on your intentions. Be generous with the details. Now is not a time to be vague about your life's desires.

When you spend quality time with your soul, you more fully recognise your innate power to create. Every idea and thought is the genesis of life — a seed awaiting the correct conditions of trust, faith and reassurance that all is unfolding and on its way. It is just a matter of time. Seeds sewn in winter flourish in springtime. Be patient and open-hearted. Feel this vision alive within every cell as a bountiful realm of endless possibility, wonder and magnificence — for you came here to dream the universe into being.

Clear intentions create plentiful and abundant manifestations. Take time to ponder your heart's intent and sacred offering for the world, even if that means an uncomfortable confrontation with something that is long overdue for a change in your life. What are your passions? What lights you up? It is time to sow the seeds of change.

GNOSIS

Remembrance. Cellular Knowing. Intuitive Pull.

In order to remember, we must acknowledge the possibility that we forgot ourselves. We must recognise that perhaps we have not truly been ourselves for a very long time.

Forgetting creates opportunities for others to tell our story for us, to influence our direction in life. Yet, every cell of your divine body holds the entire holographic universe. The galactic and universal records of all that ever was and will ever be. This is the divine intelligence of what can never be learned in books or taught in schools, for it is an internal path of remembering. The answers are within you — they always were.

Throughout the globe, the fog of amnesia is steadily dissolving, bringing more clarity with each new day. The smoke and mirrors of the world are clearing, as the great illumination reveals all that must be exposed to bring us to a new set of choice points, a newfound awareness. Your senses are attuning. Perhaps you are experiencing more vivid dreams, moments of déjà vu, or deep impressions of just knowing without being able to explain it to others. Chills up and down your spine or flutters in your stomach are signals from your body's ancient remembering. Trust your gnosis. Your body temple holds the Source of all things, the microcosm of the macrocosm. Your insight is igniting. You are remembering.

GRANDMOTHER WEAVER
Bridging Realms. Fresh Horizons. Threads of Light.

GRANDMOTHER WEAVER

Bridging Realms. Fresh Horizons.
Threads of Light.

For millennia, ancient tribal grandmothers—the original weavers of creation—have been working sacred threads of light. They have been weaving worlds, the spiritual with the physical, threading their prayers and sacred songs into a tapestry of unity, love and peace for the collective, Mother Earth and all of creation.

This is the primordial vision of healing and awakening throughout the modern world. You, too, are weaving your highest vision into reality. The warp and the weave hold steady as your commitment to love stretches your light far and wide, generously blanketing the world in a field of grace. You are spinning the fibres for your own luminous garment — which wraps you in your divine majesty. This card is a reminder to take great care with your creations. Choose threads of love and compassion for self and others. Untangle all threads of self-doubt, fear and shame. Remember, you are the creator of your reality, the weaver of your life's highest manifestation. Thread by thread, you unfold the potential for miracles in all realms. This is your vision quest. It is time to dream big.

HARMONY OF THE SPHERES

Shifting Orbit. Co-Creation. Unite with Your Community.

HARMONY OF THE SPHERES

Shifting Orbit. Co-Creation. Unite with Your Community.

As the planets orbit around the sun in their cosmic dance of the spheres, you are called to remember your place in the community. Collaboration, co-creation and connection with others is a natural expression of your soul. By honouring your uniqueness, you shine as a luminous hub of light, drenching the world in your compelling presence. Your light brings a warm glow of inspiration to the hearts of your soul family, and those from a future timeline you are yet to cross paths with.

The process of awakening need not always be introspective and lonesome; joining forces with others amplifies the light. After all, your light was always meant to be shared. Like floating orbs drifting towards each other, you are uniting with your community.

Your powerful wisdom, life experiences and soul gifts are of great magnitude, and the world is ready to listen to what you have to say. You are recognising the beauty in being seen and supported, and in allowing others to be seen and supported by you. Recently, you may have experienced big shifts in relationships and how you relate with others. You may have questioned why someone who was once so close is abruptly no longer — for you have shifted orbits. We must accept that some people only join us for part of the journey and are not destined to go the whole way.

Now is the time to clarify your values and commit to your truth, as this sends out a potent call for others to respond. Your sacred kin have heard your clarion call. Let go of the how and when, and allow synchronicity to blend miracles along the way.

HEART LOTUS

Rising from the Depths. Leadership. Pioneering the Way.

HEART LOTUS

Rising from the Depths. Leadership.
Pioneering the Way.

From deep within the muddy waters, the lotus rises into full bloom. Coded within her is the knowing of her greatness, beauty and strength. The seed of her ancient heart preserves her fullest potential. Just as the lotus draws nourishment from the depths, you, too, can rise from the darkness despite all unexpected odds. Lotus medicine reminds you that adversity, challenge and struggle are all part of the awakening journey. They are essential aspects of soul growth, initiation and mastery. How can you be equally grateful for life's blessings and struggles? Both have contributed to who you are today.

Life's many challenges have kindled your compassionate spirit, as love leads first. In a world dominated by mind and thought, you bring something different. You think with your heart, rising above any murkiness of collective thought. Now is the time to take action on projects that uplift consciousness. Be assertive as you step forward into leadership roles. You are rising into bloom, leading others to do the same in discovering their own seed of potential — their bud buried deep in the mud. It is time to pioneer the way.

HOLY SOPHIA

Self-Nurturance. The Journey Within. Self-Love.

HOLY SOPHIA

Self-Nurturance. The Journey Within. Self-Love.

You are being called to honour your feminine spirit. This is a moment for self-nourishment and introspection, to soften the edges and smooth out all within your life that is rigid and inflexible. This is an invitation to cultivate deeper intimacy with self. Have you been listening to the gentle whispers of your sacred body? Or have you perhaps been soldiering on and pushing forward? The over-productive way of being is rapidly fatiguing your spirit.

If your soul is feeling parched, it may be time to soften into the loving embrace of Holy Sophia. This card is a reminder to carve out space in your day for devotional time with yourself. As you journey inward, you rediscover the miraculous cosmos that exists within you. This is your temple of creation, echoing Holy Sophia's celestial songs — the feminine realm of grace. It is time to replenish your spirit; fill up your cup with the sweet nectars of life with effortless, bountiful glory. Serving from a cup that is low on supply causes resentment and friction with others. By tending to yourself first, you can better support others. Remember, all that you need is within you, the fountain of perpetual life force. It is time to slow down, breathe and tune in. It's okay to put yourself first.

INNER SANCTUM

Rejuvenation. Safe Sanctuary. Time to Receive.

INNER SANCTUM

Rejuvenation. Safe Sanctuary. Time to Receive.

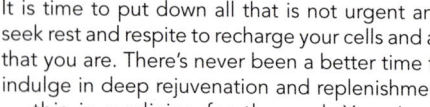

It is time to put down all that is not urgent and seek rest and respite to recharge your cells and all that you are. There's never been a better time to indulge in deep rejuvenation and replenishment — this is medicine for the soul. Your inner sanctum awaits, offering you an unlimited supply of nourishment that tends to your heart, mind, body and soul.

All too often, you have found yourself as the space holder, a pillar of strength for those needing it most. Yet these divine acts of service can be a lot to hold — for family, friends, partners and children, and for colleagues and the wider community. What advice of your own could you take? It is a powerful gesture of self-love when you can step back from it all and retreat to be embraced by your own sacred space.

By giving yourself permission to move inward, you become a priority in your own life. By honouring your own needs, your inner flame ignites, blazing brighter the more you tend to it. If we let our fire fade to ashes, it takes a greater investment of energy to revive it. Now is a time to honour your own needs, to acknowledge your longing for space and quality time in quiet contemplation. This is also a perfect time to receive nurturance from those who wish to support you. It is in this way that your devotional acts of care and kindness return to you with warm blessings.

LIQUID LIGHT

Adaptability. Flexibility. Flow.

LIFTING THE VEIL

Clear Vision. Illumination. Higher Mind.

Veils are lifting, and new truths are coming to light. You are called to welcome change, as much of life is being stirred up. Trust that everything is working for you. The universe is re-organising itself, catapulting you into deep awareness of your soul's miraculous potential. Fresh possibilities are upon you that were previously out of reach.

It is time to release outdated stories, behaviours, habits and distractions that are stifling your inner radiance. Are there masks and facades that no longer align with your authentic spirit? Your perspective and values are shifting. A re-evaluation of self may be in the highest order. In this moment, what feels out of sync with your higher soul's calling? What new choices resonate with your unique inner truth, regardless of others? Listen to this quiet voice. Not all that shimmers and glistens is always as it seems. You pierce through the veil, seeing through the filters that would normally obscure your access to what is truly available to you.

This card confirms that you are expanding in consciousness; your senses are attuning as you read between the lines. In your rising, all is illuminated by the light. Trust the ancient wisdom of your soul's knowing. Release attachments of wanting something to be a certain way when the energetics don't add up. You are divinely guided every step of the way.

LUMINOUS WATERS
Purification. The Deep Freeze Is Melting.

LIQUID LIGHT

Adaptability. Flexibility. Flow.

As the rigid structures of the world dissolve, you are being called into a new state. What once seemed so solid and permanent is becoming more fluid. A great 'osmosis' is underway as realities blend into one another. As insights flow, new opportunities present themselves.

This is a period of great plasticity in your life, presenting the perfect time to make necessary changes. A moment to adapt, reshape and remould your sense of self. Be intentional with the energies you choose to surround yourself with. In your home, work or personal life, your environment either supports you or constrains you. It can hold you in love, or it can constrict your flow.

Flexibility enables you to ride the waves of change. You are called to be like water. You are the formlessness within a form, the liquid within the solid. Your spirit is a wellspring of energy, held within your body's sacred vessel. You are here to overflow with radiant love as your surplus graces the path of many around you. Releasing the 'cup-half-empty' mindset inspires a positive outlook to motivate your journey. Appreciation maximises the flow.

LIFTING THE VEIL

Clear Vision. Illumination. Higher Mind.

LUMINOUS WATERS

Purification. The Deep Freeze Is Melting.

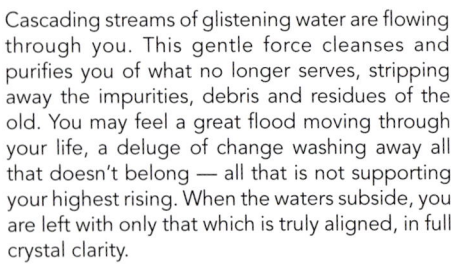

Cascading streams of glistening water are flowing through you. This gentle force cleanses and purifies you of what no longer serves, stripping away the impurities, debris and residues of the old. You may feel a great flood moving through your life, a deluge of change washing away all that doesn't belong — all that is not supporting your highest rising. When the waters subside, you are left with only that which is truly aligned, in full crystal clarity.

Divine Mother's waters are supporting your journey. She is the amniotic ocean, the cosmic substance holding all life. She nurtures your flourishing and greatest becoming. You are reminded that water holds memory, as it is a medium for consciousness. It is our ancient ancestor, for we, too, are bodies of water.

This sacred element is emitting new information, codes of intelligent energy that hold new potentials. You are moving through deep soul healing, and this is being felt on a cellular level. Painful traumas cause a deep freeze, imprinting memories that cause hardness, blockages and even physical discomfort. You may have felt stiff or stuck in idle, wanting to move forward on your soul mission, but with your body holding back in distrust. Fears, apprehension or doubts produce a heavy weight you have carried for far too long.

At this time, much is transforming and quickening, catalysing you forth. The warmth of the new era is upon us; the deep freeze is melting, thawing out all that is ready to be released. It is time to bask in the glistening flows and invigorate your spirit!

MIRACLE CREATION
Holding the Vision. Birthing the New.

MIRACLE CREATION

Holding the Vision. Birthing the New.

Creativity is the highest expression of the divine; it is the source of universal love and cosmic intelligence. This abundant energy awakens your body, mind, heart and soul, igniting curiosity and wonder in every moment — the delicate scent of a rose, a drop of rain upon your cheek, the gentle breeze upon your skin … Your soul is filled with the fertile dimension of Source itself, the intimate union with the substance of all life.

You hold the power for creation. It is written and woven into your soul's blueprint. You are being called to reflect upon your journey. Have you crafted with great intention and care? Or has auto-pilot living taken over? Do you feel awed by your life's masterpiece, or do you know you're destined for more? You may feel your visions, dreams and goals are getting stuck in the birth canal. It is time to breathe, to trust the innate capacity within you.

You are an active creator of the New Earth. Every seed that you cultivate contributes to the cosmic biodiversity of life. The easy route of replicating others' creations is a missed opportunity for you to shine. The world needs your originality, your ideas and your unique signature. It is time to believe in yourself, to honour your own existence and the magnificence of creation all around you. This is your divine legacy. It is time to birth the new.

OCEANIC GUARDIANS

Spirit Guardians. Rites of Passage.

OCEANIC GUARDIANS

Spirit Guardians. Rites of Passage.

It is time to receive support. You do not have to do it all alone. You may be feeling the intensities of deep soul growth as you migrate to expanded realities. This spiritual uplevelling is challenging everything you once thought you knew, all that once felt secure and permanent. The voyage of leaving one state of being and migrating to another is what you came here for. Change and expansion are the only constants. Stasis is no longer an option. The majestic guardians of the oceans are riding with you, accompanying you to higher realms. They are the protectors and gatekeepers of your heart, and their presence reminds you to trust in the unknown. Soothe your inner waters by immersing in their sound bath of love. For you, too, are a water being. You began by breathing water in your mother's womb, blissfully floating in her luminal ocean, shapeshifting into your miraculous form.

The whales and dolphins are ancient beings from Sirius, supporting humankind in their greatest transformation yet. Their sonic tones disperse loving energy through all bodies of water and vast seas. As the medium for their telepathy, water conveys the vision of their sacred prayer. You are guided into the next octave of your journey through their safe passage. It is time to soften in deep trust and swim among the cosmic seas — to dive right in and glide gracefully to expanded horizons. The guardians are with you; you are held by the pod.

OPHIUCHUS

Soul Retrieval. Calling in Support.

OPHIUCHUS

Soul Retrieval. Calling in Support.

You are reminded that spiritual awakening need not be arduous and gruelling — it can be a joyful and pleasant journey. How can you view hurdles and challenges as initiations? How do they expand your awareness of self? It is time to stop resisting the discomfort. Instead, lean in.

Soften into the wisdom of pain and trust that if it's speaking louder, it's time to listen. You are ready to retrieve parts of you that were left behind, parts that were forgotten, fractured or frozen in stasis. When we have the courage to lean into our discomfort, we build strong self-trust. Rather than escaping it, we lend a listening ear and an open heart. We allow it to come forward into a safe space. Tending to open wounds requires a healing field of compassion and understanding. You do not need to do it all alone. Call upon your healing teams and divine guides to hold you in an aura of soothing light. Request prayers when you need extra support and ask others to assist when you need it most. During times of crisis, we can be cracked open in unimaginable ways. There is light at the end of the dark tunnel. But the way is not around it; it's through it.

OUROBOROS

Self-Sufficiency. Eternal Cycles. Death and Rebirth.

OUROBOROS

Self-Sufficiency. Eternal Cycles.
Death and Rebirth.

All that you need is within you, for you are the embodiment of all that is. Searching for answers outside of yourself is a great constrictor, as it limits your potential for expansion.

The journey of life is an eternal cycle of death and rebirth, of destruction and re-creation. Your skin is shedding, and old layers are peeling away as your new, glistening self emerges.

All things—material and spiritual—are unified and never truly disappear; they cycle back around in a different form. The ouroboros, the ring of fire, is the kundalini of your spirit that flows in eternal motion, energising your greatest rising. Creative, sensual eros pulses life force through your entire being. This is the Source that lives and breathes through you.

Remember that your greatest power comes from within you, not from outside of you. If you have depended upon other people or a power outside of yourself, it may be time to coil up like the great serpent and move inward. Unwind the mind as you journey inward, discovering where you have lost faith in your own inner connection. Replenish yourself from the inside out to draw upon your unlimited supply. With deep renewal, you radiate your brightest light.

PEARL OF LIGHT

Inner Child. Innocence. Presence in the Now.

PEARL OF LIGHT

Inner Child. Innocence. Presence in the Now.

Your essence is sacred. You are treasured and held dearly in the vastness of love — the infinite ocean of consciousness.

Over the years, you may have found it difficult to connect to your inner child. You may have lost sight of your pearl of light and the innocence within you. Has your joyous, playful and curious spirit been traded for a life of seriousness?

Leaving our inner children behind, we mould ourselves into a modern world, a place that has forgotten what is truly valuable. Instead of flowing with imagination, we calculate and over-plan, attempting to feel secure. We trade our spontaneous spirit with predictability, censoring our whimsical spirit with our rational mind. By doing so, we may lose touch with the powerful present moment and the freedom of simplicity. Our carefree childhood years may become a long-lost memory.

If you have been inundated with life's rigorous demands, it may be time to rediscover your pearl of light — your luminous inner child, glowing within. By appreciating the magic of creation, even the most mundane tasks can be brought to life! Carve out space for impromptu adventures that shake up your routine as you invite creativity to take the lead.

SHIELDING

Protection. Boundaries. Sovereign Space.

SHIELDING

Protection. Boundaries. Sovereign Space.

As a highly empathic soul, you feel deeply. The heartache of the world impacts you in ways that may feel overwhelming at times. Sensitivity is a true gift of the human experience. To walk in another's shoes enables you to hold deep compassion and empathy. Without this, we become numb, disconnected and apathetic towards life.

In order to shine your most radiant light, your energy must be balanced and vitalised; your aura must be bright. Yet with your open heart, it's important to be discerning — to recognise what's yours to hold and what's not. Carrying burdens for others causes great depletion, as does spreading yourself too thin. We cannot give what we don't have, or we can end up fatigued. If you have been over-giving or leaking your energy, time and resources, you may need to step back from it all to take stock of your habits and patterns.

On the other hand, if you are meticulously over-armouring yourself, fearful of intruders and in protection mode everywhere you go, you may be overdoing it. Being defensive, expecting the worst to happen or harbouring intense scepticism can dilute your connection with others and the alluring beauty of life. Trust in the power within you. Lead with love as your greatest shield of all.

STARGATE

Portal to the Divine. Standing at the Threshold.

STARGATE

Portal to the Divine. Standing at the Threshold.

A doorway is opening. It is already ajar. What lies on the other side is the unknown, the future version of your soul. You have reached the threshold, and a new door is opening — an initiation of change and metamorphosis.

Initially, feelings of hesitation may arise as you hold on to what's familiar, for if you step through the portal, you are guaranteed to change. What's on the other side may be out of focus, blurry and unclear. Yet you will never know the true beauty and miracle of life if you don't first trust.

This is what's at stake. But you are ready. You have successfully passed through many other thresholds, great shifts that have taken place in your life. Like stepping stones, they have paved the way, guiding you to this point today.

Closing the door on important opportunities may leave you feeling conflicted. You may feel they have slipped through your fingers. Trust that if doors are opening, it's at the hand of your soul. Your job is to trust and follow the guidance of your higher self. It is time to walk through into your greatest becoming.

STARSEED

Ancient Origins. Soul Mission. Higher Purpose.

STARSEED

Ancient Origins. Soul Mission. Higher Purpose.

Do you wonder where your true origins lie? Do you often look to the stars, galaxies and universal realms for answers? During this time of awakening, you may be feeling a deep longing to reunite with your galactic family and the cosmic realms.

As a Starseed, your spiritual gifts may have been downplayed as a child. You might've felt pressured to adapt to the world. You may have unknowingly concealed your powers and gifts to avoid rejection or judgement from others. Yet, even with the challenges of fitting into family and society, you still feel a deep love for humanity, for you volunteered on this mission to shine your light. You are medicine for this awakening world. You are here to preserve the earth and uplift humanity, and this is what drives you the most.

You are here for a great purpose. You hold ancient–future wisdom, igniting your path through the haze of a sleeping world. The responsibility you feel can cause pressure at times, with your expanded heart called to support many divine causes. It may be time to break the mission down into smaller pieces. Move one small step at a time. One stepping stone leads to the next, and you do not need to have it all figured out right now — all will be revealed in divine timing. Meanwhile, your mission is alive in all the daily gestures of kindness and love you offer the world.

TEMPLE OF LIGHT

Silver Lining. Second Chances. The Blank Slate.

A big part of the human journey is making 'mistakes'. It is the way we learn, grow and expand as we become increasingly self-aware and empowered. In fact, mistakes are amazing opportunities.

As you reflect and get clear on your deepest values, you can shape the kind of person you wish to be. In a universe that doesn't hold grudges, you are reminded that it's okay to be human. You are loved just the same. Flaws, shortcomings and imperfections (as you might see it) are witnessed through the eyes of love.

This card is a reminder to be kind to yourself. Know that second chances are dawning; the silver lining is peaking through spaces of turbulent darkness. If you feel uneasy about the past or your actions towards another, now is the time for unwavering compassion. Trust that all is forgiven, and it's time to now forgive yourself. This is often the hardest part; release the burden of guilt and shame and let go. Forgive. The temple of light is calling you. The blank slate is here.

THE DEEP DESCENT

Subconscious. Underworld. Excavating the Old.

In a world where many focus on their best angle, you are here to radiate your most authentic self. In over-emphasising perfection, you may unknowingly conceal the raw and vulnerable aspects of yourself.

When things are going swell, we have a spring in our step and tend to be more outward with our energy. We like to be witnessed in our stride. When we have everything together, we feel on top of the world. This is the external perception we have been taught is so important to maintain.

However, buoying upon the water's surface, the iceberg is just a small part of the picture. Beneath the surface exists a much larger domain of unconscious thoughts and beliefs. This is the deeper dimension of ourselves, the storage centre for our shadows and traumas — the heavy, weighted emotions that lurk beneath the surface.

Wearing masks and hiding your pain, fears and insecurities from others denies your radical authenticity. No longer must you suffer behind closed doors. Your honest, raw self is an inspiration for a healing world. By being vulnerable and giving yourself permission to seek help, you inspire others to do the same. Now is a time of deep descent — an inward pilgrimage of tender healing, the journey of acknowledging all parts of self, including the light, the dark and all in between. It's okay to not have everything together, to be seen in your unravelling and unpolished state. You are worthy. You are loved.

THE EYE OF THE STORM

Peace. Centredness Amidst Great Change.

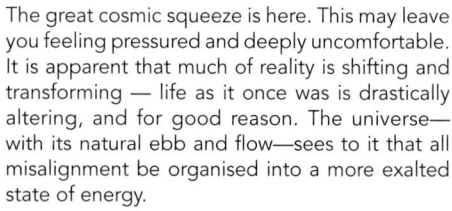

The great cosmic squeeze is here. This may leave you feeling pressured and deeply uncomfortable. It is apparent that much of reality is shifting and transforming — life as it once was is drastically altering, and for good reason. The universe— with its natural ebb and flow—sees to it that all misalignment be organised into a more exalted state of energy.

You are being supported to hold your centre as the great storm shakes up emotions, fears and insecurities, agitating the atmosphere of your reality. There must first be an undoing and dismantling before the dust settles and you can see clearly. It is time to soften into the sweet spot of your heart—your steady, inner knowing—when all else is whirling around you. This may mean stepping back from certain aspects of life that are diminishing your inner peace or pulling you into a vortex of worry or anxiety.

The great winds of revelation are here, sifting through all you once believed to be true, allowing a new perspective to appear. You are being called into the eye of the storm — your radiant heart, where harmony, trust and surrender shelter you from the chaos. This is the still point of eternal truth, the acceptance that all is well and it is okay to let go. Trust in the unravelling. The new is stirring in the air.

THE GREAT ATTRACTORS

Magnetism. Manifestation Power.
The Cosmic Pull.

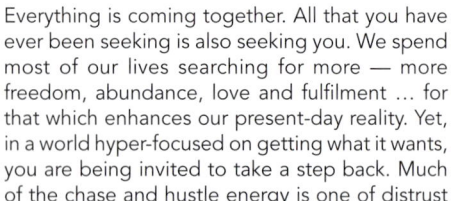

Everything is coming together. All that you have ever been seeking is also seeking you. We spend most of our lives searching for more — more freedom, abundance, love and fulfilment … for that which enhances our present-day reality. Yet, in a world hyper-focused on getting what it wants, you are being invited to take a step back. Much of the chase and hustle energy is one of distrust and impatience. It is one of escaping or avoiding the current conditions of life.

You are reminded of your powerful magnetism. The intelligent language of the universe pulls your dreams, desires and greatest imaginings towards you. Your job is to be a vibrational match to your dreams. If you wish to experience more love, how can you first love yourself? If you wish to experience more abundance, how can you feel prosperous right now, with things being exactly as they are? If we wait for something to manifest to feel differently about ourselves, it may likely never come to be.

The dialogue of the universe is one of correspondence. It is the cosmic conversation, fluxing and dancing in a call-and-response with our higher self. Just like a radio station, we must 'dial' our frequency to hear the music of our soul. We must be a matching vibration. It is time to let go of pushing and invite magnetism to do the talking.

THE HOLY GRAIL

Sacred Lineage. Sisterhood. Priestess Lines.

THE HOLY GRAIL

Sacred Lineage. Sisterhood. Priestess Lines.

You are the keeper of creation codes. Your inner sanctum connects you beyond the veil. Your deep reverence for creation reflects your elegant grace and beauty, for you are the portal of creation.

For many years, women have put up towering walls to cope in a patriarchal world. Being in defence—although it protects us—keeps us stiff and heavy. Our armour becomes clumsy and impedes our ability to move freely.

Yet, the fear of being seen by others or attracting unwanted attention is a memory that lives on in many. To this day, fully standing in your truth, spiritual gifts and power may ignite feelings of concern and unease. You may find yourself hesitating to step forward, worried about shining too brightly. Your mind says yes, but your body says no — an inner conflict brewing within.

It is time to feel into these inhibitions and that which is holding you back. Healing unresolved wounds from the past supports you in reclaiming your wise, empowered self, filling you with the flowing grace of the divine. You are restoring faith in your own power — the beacon of light you are in the world. You are called to uncover your innermost truth, your deepest longing for freedom. As you feel safe to let down your guard, your sacred sisters stand with you, pouring into you with their loving support. Take a breath as you find your divine stride. The Holy Grail is within you.

THE VISIONARY

The Future Is Here. Beyond the Veil.

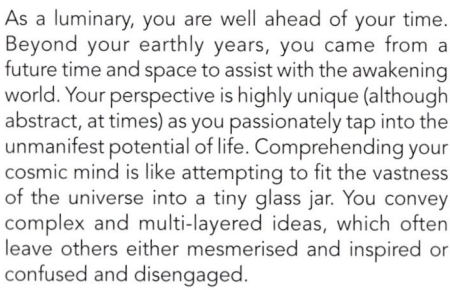

As a luminary, you are well ahead of your time. Beyond your earthly years, you came from a future time and space to assist with the awakening world. Your perspective is highly unique (although abstract, at times) as you passionately tap into the unmanifest potential of life. Comprehending your cosmic mind is like attempting to fit the vastness of the universe into a tiny glass jar. You convey complex and multi-layered ideas, which often leave others either mesmerised and inspired or confused and disengaged.

You see into the potential of what could be, bringing clarity to the foggy cloud of amnesia. As waves of incarnating souls like you are reaching Earth, the glass ceiling is dissolving. You hold a clear vantage of what is possible. Your lucidity is heightening as the dreaming realms become manifest. In accessing the bigger picture, you represent a new way forward. Hold faith in your heart, for the beauty and magic of your visions are steadily anchoring on the earth plane.

All will be revealed in due course. It is time to honour your psychic gifts and continue to sharpen your tools of discernment. In this way, the path ahead becomes clearer, and you can more fully assist others.

TIMELINE JUMP
Course Correction. A New Trajectory Is Unfolding.

TIMELINE JUMP

Course Correction. A New Trajectory
Is Unfolding.

Old realities are collapsing. Past connections, friendships, careers and outdated ways of being are dismantling as new pathways emerge. New horizons are upon you. This is your opportunity to quantum leap, to recognise that the comfort of the past may be stifling your greatest rising. New energies are available and are highly magnified, igniting your courageous spirit to leap into the unknown.

Cultivating inner peace aligns you with your highest trajectory. Take one step at a time; breathe and find your footing. As the inertia builds, allow magnetism to guide you. While standing at a crossroads, you are staring down the barrel of vastly different life paths. Trust the pull; seize the moment and make the first move. Take action on your heart's deepest desires and that which lights you up. Allow logic to take a back seat — this doesn't need to make sense.

You attune to your higher timeline by acting upon passion, joy and excitement. When you harbour fear, doubt and scarcity, your path becomes a vibrational match. Freedom is a choice to be made. It can be felt in every divine breath, as each inhalation gifts a new possibility.

Regardless of the paths of others, commit to staying in your lane — the authenticity of your soul will guide you faithfully. You may even be pleasantly surprised with what emerges! You are being lifted into a new octave, but you must intentionally choose it. It is time to course correct.

TREE OF LIFE

Stabilise Your Roots. Honour the Seasons.

Trees with established roots expand the furthest into the skies; their firm base sustains their fractal branching as their shimmering leaves dance freely in the breeze, achieving maximum reach. Those trees that speedily shoot up without first descending downward become dainty and easily blown over by the next storm.

The nature of life is growth. Instinctively, we seek expansion to elevate our sense of self and thrive in the ecosystem of life. Yet the wisdom of trees reminds you that laying foundations is equally important. In fact, your growth depends on it.

The deeper your grounding, the greater your rising. Tending to your earthly, physical needs, like adequate rest and nutrition, upholds your towering ascent. Piercing through the canopy above requires careful attention and conditioning of the soil below.

If you have been consistently seeking out your next activation or spiritual breakthrough, it may be time to retreat and honour a time of integration — to firmly anchor into your roots. Check in with your physical self: Do I feel over-stimulated and frazzled? Is my body playing catch up, feeling fatigued and sluggish, adjusting to the influx of higher frequencies? Honour your seasons, phases of prolific growth and deep rest. Patience is key. Increment by increment, like growth rings inside a tree, you are expanding at the very core of your being. Remember, your spirituality includes your physicality. You do not need to choose one state over the other. As above, so below.

About the Artist & Author

Katrina Smith is a celebrated ascension guide, spiritual luminary, visionary artist and devoted mother. Through her deep commitment to an awakening world, she guides others into profound transformation and self-empowerment. She recognises that every being holds within them the totality of all things — an internal access and birthright of epic magnitude. She facilitates transformative healing spaces to support her clients in retrieving and recognising their own divine aspects and embodying their most exalted timeline.

Her visionary artworks are transmissions and activations of the eternal realms of consciousness beyond the veil. Her greatest vision and heart's intention is to awaken all willing hearts to the knowing of their own unique potential. A world where all recognise their own divinity is a world thriving in abundant love and harmony.

@katrinasmithofficial
katrinasmith.me

Also available from Blue Angel®

MESSAGES OF ANGELS
Heavenly Wisdom & Support

Anna Grace Taylor • Artwork by Parita Naran

Wrap yourself in the warmth of your angels' wings with this uplifting oracle deck by renowned Angel Therapist Anna Grace Taylor. Whether seeking answers to questions in your heart or simply a dose of daily reassurance, these cards illuminate your path with wise words and gentle support. Cultivate a space of peace and clarity, knowing your angels are always by your side.

50 cards + instruction card • ISBN: 978-1-922574-52-7

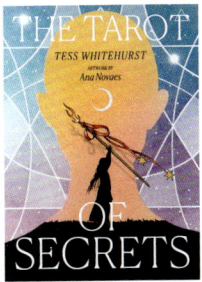

THE TAROT OF SECRETS
A formulary, catalyst, and key
Tess Whitehurst • Artwork by Ana Novaes

The Tarot of Secrets, from renowned author Tess Whitehurst, offers the formula to unlock and embody universal mysteries through your own transcendent DNA. Artist Ana Novaes re-imagines Tarot for the 21st century, weaving together traditional esoteric symbolism and everyday experience to produce an evocative deck that will be loved by novices and collectors alike.

78 Cards & Guidebook • ISBN: 978-1-922574-45-9

Notes